PRAISE FOR THE SINGING

Songs for Children

COLLECTED BY

MADELAINE GILL

and

GREG PLISKA

Illustrated by MADELAINE GILL
Arrangements by GREG PLISKA

Little, Brown and Company
Boston Toronto London

Acknowledgments

I would like to thank the following people for helping me in the research for this book:
Margorie King Barab at All Souls Unitarian Church, Barbara Hemmings at Riverside Church,
Tova Ronni at the Tarbuth Foundation, Elizabeth Childs, Natalie Sleeth, Reverend Bruce Anderson,
and Anne Gill.

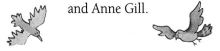

I am particularly grateful to Father Michael Kuhn at the Emmanuel Church for singing many of these songs in
Chapel at the Cathedral School, and for his enthusiastic spirit. I am also grateful to Joan Edward for her singing
and recording of the songs, and to all the children at the Cathedral School for their singing as well.

Finally, I want to express my appreciation to John Keller for suggesting the idea for this book, and my
thanks to Karen Klockner, Susan Lu, and Jackie Horne for shepherding it along and turning it into a book.
Amen.

M. G.

Illustrations and compilation of songs copyright © 1993 by Madelaine Gill
Musical arrangements and compilation of songs copyright © 1993 by Greg Pliska

First Edition

Copyright acknowledgments appear on page 64.

Library of Congress Cataloging-in-Publication Data
Praise for the singing : songs for children / collected by Madelaine Gill
and Greg Pliska ; illustrated by Madelaine Gill ; arrangements by Greg Pliska.
— 1st ed.
1 score
Summary: An illustrated collection of hymns that can be used in the home
or any ecumenical setting
ISBN 0-316-52627-4
1. Hymns, English — Juvenile. [1. Hymns.] I. Gill, Madelaine.
II. Pliska, Greg.
M2193.P77 1993   91-750562

10 9 8 7 6 5 4 3 2 1

IM

Published simultaneously in Canada by Little, Brown & Company (Canada) Limited

Printed in Hong Kong

For my mother, Anne Barnard Gill, and her beautiful voice singing the Doxology
at Sunday lunch, at supper in the summer, and on every other Special Occasion.

M. G.

To Vladimir and Gigi, who lit the spark; Mom and Dad, who tended the flame; Dawn, who tends the fire;
and the many young people to whom the torch is passed.

G. P.

PREFACE

The songs in this book come from various traditions and cultures. They include African-American spirituals, American folk songs, church hymns, Shaker songs, and songs of Jewish origin. Some of the tunes are several hundred years old and some are contemporary. The words in a few of the songs have been changed to enrich them with meaning for the world we live in today. The history of hymnody, like the history of all creation, is one of change.

The song arrangements attempt to bridge the traditional and the contemporary. A livelier rhythm, a new harmonic twist, an expanded accompaniment pattern — all are intended to provide new perspectives on familiar melodies. The arrangements provide a balance of difficulty levels, to challenge the novice and to provide the veteran with an opportunity for expressiveness not found in standard hymnals. A number of the songs feature rounds and part singing; others may be sung in call-and-response form. Clapping along, occasionally notated, is always welcome. Dance — the symbol of creation in many cultures — is inextricably linked to music; parents, teachers, and group leaders should encourage movement whenever teaching or singing these songs

The songs are grouped by theme: Joy and Celebration, Peace and Freedom, Hope and Faith, and Love and Thanksgiving. In choosing them, we looked for songs whose melodies and images would appeal to children. Each song expresses the power and wonder of faith.

In the end, these arrangements and illustrations should be for you what the original songs were for us: springboards for creativity. We hope that this collection will be used not only as a resource but also as an inspiration to "look up, and laugh and love and lift,"* and, above all, to sing.

Madelaine Gill   *Greg Pliska*

*from "I Would Be True"

CONTENTS

Joy and Celebration

Peace and Freedom

Hope and Faith

Love and Thanksgiving

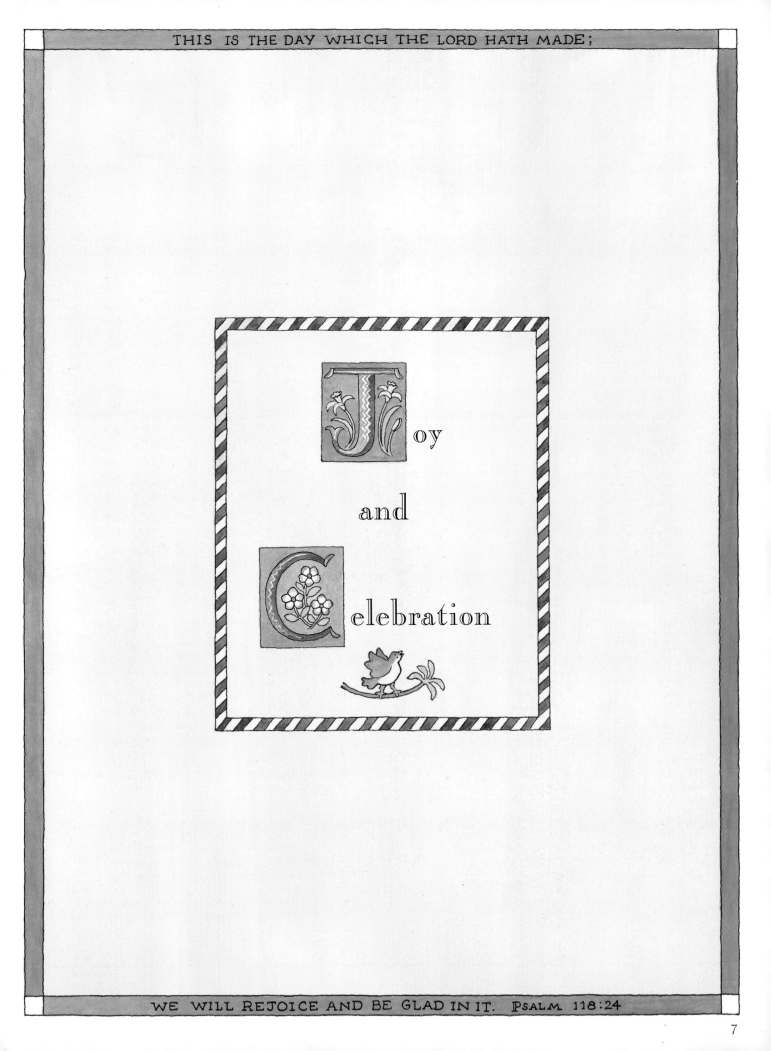

Joy and Celebration

Morning Has Broken

Eleanor Farjeon

Old Gaelic Melody

Flowingly

1. Morn-ing has bro - ken like the first morn - ing;
2. Mine is the sun - light, mine is the morn - ing,

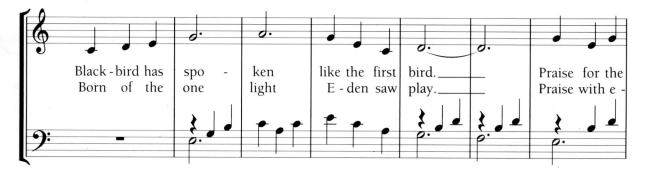

Black-bird has spo - ken like the first bird. Praise for the
Born of the one light E - den saw play. Praise with e -

sing - ing, praise for the morn - ing, Praise for them spring -
la - tion, praise ev-'ry morn - ing, God's re - cre - a -

ing fresh from the word.
tion of the new day.

The Canticle of the Sun

Francis of Assisi
Tr. William H. Draper

Old German Melody

Staidly

Verse

1. All crea-tures of the earth and sky, With
2. Thou rush-ing wind that art so strong, Ye

glad-ness lift your voic-es high, Al-le-lu-ia, al-le-lu-ia! Thou
clouds that sail in heav'n a-long, Al-le-lu-ia, al-le-lu-ia! Thou

burn-ing sun with gol-den beam, Thou sil-ver moon with soft-er
ris-ing morn, in praise re-joice; Ye lights of eve-ning, find a

Chorus

gleam, Oh,___ praise God, oh,___ praise God, Al-le-
voice.

lu-ia, al-le-lu-ia, al-le-lu-ia!

Holy, Holy, Holy

Reginald Heber
William Channing Gannet

John Bacchus Dykes

Legato

1. Ho - ly, ho - ly, ho - ly, Lord,__ God Al - might - y!
2. Bring, O morn, thy mu - sic; night, thy star - lit si - lence.

Ear - ly in the morn - ing our song shall rise to Thee.
O - ceans, laugh the rap - ture to the storm winds cours - ing free.

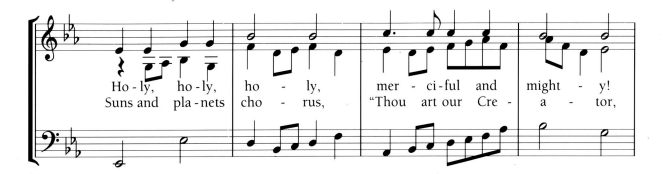

Ho - ly, ho - ly, ho - ly, mer - ci - ful and might - y!
Suns and pla - nets cho - rus, "Thou art our Cre - a - tor,

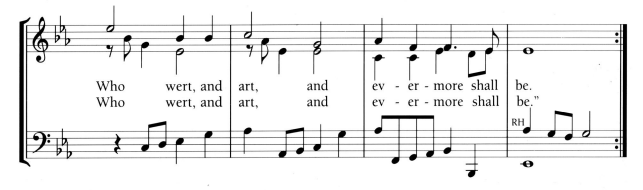

Who wert, and art, and ev - er - more shall be.
Who wert, and art, and ev - er - more shall be."

RH

And God created great whales, and every living creature that moveth,
which the waters brought forth abundantly, after their kind...

Genesis 1:21

Sing Hosanna

Traditional

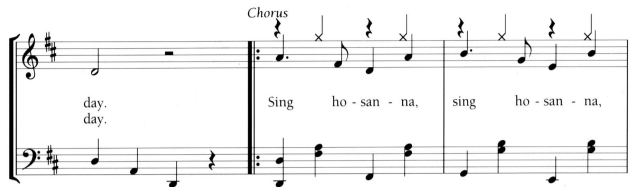

Chorus

day.
day.

Sing ho - san - na, sing ho - san - na,

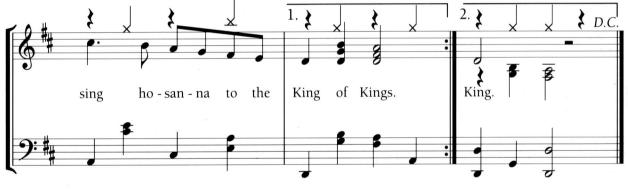

sing ho - san - na to the King of Kings.

1.

2.

D.C.

King.

And God said, Let the waters bring forth
abundantly the moving creature that hath
life, and fowl *that* may fly above the earth
in the open firmament of heaven. Genesis 1:20

Joyful, Joyful, We Adore Thee

Henry van Dyke

Ludwig van Beethoven

With feeling

1. Joy-ful, joy-ful, we a-dore Thee, God of glo-ry, God of love;
2. All Thy works with joy sur-round Thee; earth and heav'n re - flect Thy rays.

And God made the beast of the earth after his kind, and cattle after their kind, and every thing that creepeth upon the earth after his kind... Genesis 1:25

Hearts un-fold like flow'rs be-fore Thee, hail Thee as the sun a - bove.
Stars and plan-ets sing a-round Thee, cen - ter of un - bro - ken praise.

Melt the clouds of sin and_ sad - ness; drive the___ dark of doubt a -way;
Field and for - est, vale and_ moun - tain, blos -som -ing mead -ow, flash -ing sea,

Giv - er of im - mor-tal glad-ness, fill us with the light of day.
Chant -ing bird and flow -ing foun-tain, call us to re - joice in Thee.

Sanctus

Traditional

Brightly

May be sung in call-and-response form.

Ho - ly, ho - ly, ho - ly, God of pow-er and might.

Heav - en and ___ earth are full of ___ Your glo-ry.

Sing ho - san - na, sing ho - san - na,

sing ho - san - na, sing al - le - lu - ia.

Alleluia

Traditional

Moderately

Al -le - lu, al-le-lu, al-le- lu, al-le-lu-ia, praise ye the Lord. Al-le

1.

2. Lord. *Fine* Praise ye the Lord, al - le - lu - ia, praise ye the

Lord, al -le -lu - ia. Praise ye the Lord, al -le -lu - ia, praise ye the

D.C. al fine

Lord. Al - le -

Praise God with the sound of the trumpet: praise him with the psaltery and harp. Psalm 150:3

Lord of the Dance

Sydney Carter · Traditional

As a celebration

1. "I danced in the morn-ing when the world was be-gun, And I danced in the moon and the stars___ and the sun, And I came down from heav-en and I danced on the earth. At Beth-le-hem I___ had my birth."

2. "I danced for the scribes___ and the phar-i-sees, But___ they would not dance and they would not fol-low me; I___ danced for the fish-er-men, for James and___ John; They came to me, and the Dance went on."

Chorus

"Dance, dance, where-ev-er you may be; I am the Lord of the

Dance," said he, "And I'll lead you all, where-ev-er you may be, And I'll

D.C.

lead you all in the Dance," said he.

3. "I danced on the Sabbath and I cured the lame;
   The holy people said it was a shame;
   They whipped me and they stripped me and they
      hung me high,
   And they left me there on a cross to die."

4. "I danced on a Friday when the sky turned black.
   It's hard to dance with the devil on your back.
   They buried my body and they thought I'd gone,
   But I am the Dance, and I still go on."

5. "They cut me down and I leapt up high;
   I am the life that'll never, never die;
   I'll live in you if you live in me.
   I am the Lord of the Dance," said he.

Praise God, from Whom All Blessings Flow

Michael Kuhn
Thomas Ken

Genevan Psalter

Peace and Freedom

Zum Gali Gali

Peace Is for All People;

All People Are for Peace

Israeli Folk Song

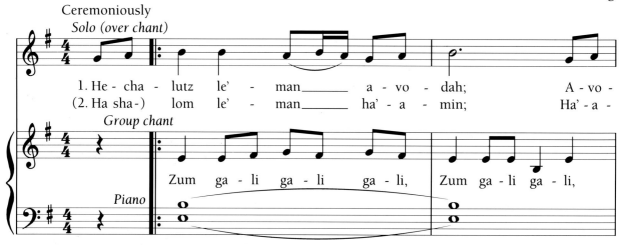

Ceremoniously

Solo (over chant)

1. He - cha - lutz le' - man_____ a - vo - dah;   A - vo -
(2. Ha sha-) lom le' - man_____ ha' - a - min;   Ha' - a -

Group chant

Zum ga - li ga - li ga - li,   Zum ga - li ga - li,

Piano

dah le' - man_____ he - cha - lutz.   2. Ha sha -
min le' - man_____ ha sha - lom.

Zum ga - li ga - li ga - li,   Zum ga - li ga - li.

Translation:
1. We will work and sing, everyone.   2. We will work till our task is done.

Hevenu Shalom Alechem

We Bring You Greetings of Peace

Traditional

With spirit

He-ve-nu sha - lom a - le-chem, he-ve-nu sha - lom a - le-chem, He-ve-nu sha - lom a - le-chem, he-ve-nu sha-lom, sha-lom, sha-lom a - le-chem.

Jerusalem

I will lift up mine eyes unto the hills,
from whence cometh my help. Psalm 121:1

23

Go Down, Moses

African-American Spiritual

Slowly
Verse

1. When Is - rael was in E - gypt's land, shall they toil, "Let my peo - ple
2. No more in bond - age "Let my peo - ple

go!" Op - pressed so hard they could not stand, "Let my peo - ple
go!" Let them come out with E - gypt's spoil, "Let my peo - ple

Chorus

go!"
go!"
"Go down, Mo - ses, way down in E - gypt's land,_____ Tell___ old___ Phar - aoh to let my peo-ple go."

And the Angel of the Lord appeared unto him in a flame of fire out of the midst of a bush: and he looked, and, behold, the bush burned with fire and the bush was not consumed.
Exodus 3:2

Dayenu

It Would Have Been Enough

The Seder Plate

Traditional

With spirit

1. I - lu ho - tci, ho - tci o - nu; ho - tci o - nu mi - Mitz - ra - yim;
2. I - lu no - san, no - san lo - nu; no - san lo - nu es ha - Sha - bos;

ho - tci o - nu mi - Mitz - ra - yim, da - ye - nu.
No - san lo - nu es ha - Sha - bos, da - ye - nu.

Chorus

Da - da - ye - nu,____

Why is this night different from all other nights?

da - da - ye-nu,_____ da - da - ye-nu, da- ye-nu, da - ye-nu._____

2. ye-nu, da - ye - nu!

LH   D.C.

Translation:
1. Had he [Moses] done nothing more than take us out of Egypt, it would have been enough.
2. Had he given us the Sabbath and nothing more, it would have been enough.

We Shall Overcome

Zilphia Horton, Frank Hamilton,
Guy Carawan, Pete Seeger

With conviction

1. We shall o - ver - come,_____ We shall o - ver - come,_____
2. We'll walk hand in hand,_____ We'll walk hand in hand,_____

We shall o - ver - come some - day._____ Oh,__
We'll walk hand in hand some - day._____ Oh,__

deep in my heart, I do be - lieve,
deep in my heart, I do be - lieve,

mf We shall o - ver - come some - day. _____
We'll walk hand in hand some - some - day. _____

RH

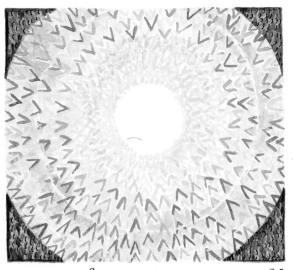

The night is far spent, the day is at hand:
let us therefore cast off works of darkness,
And let us put on the armour of light. Romans 13:12

Michael, Row the Boat Ashore

Unto a land flowing with milk and honey.   Exodus 3:8

Traditional   African-American Spiritual

With deep feeling

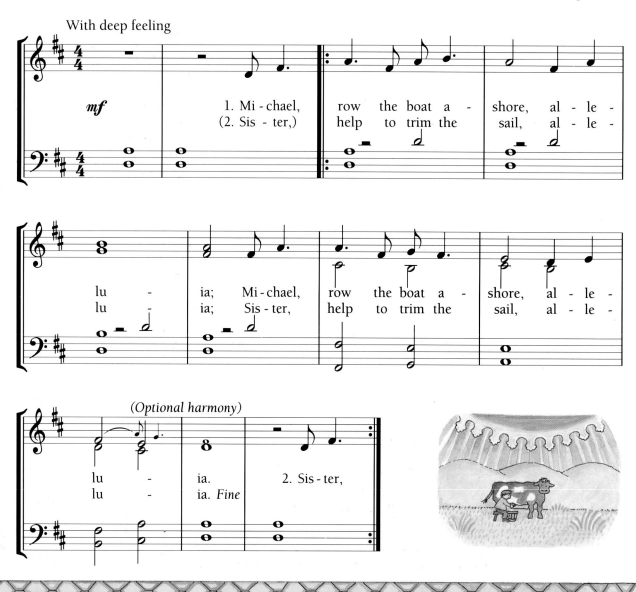

mf

1. Mi - chael,   row   the boat a -   shore,   al - le -
(2. Sis - ter,)   help   to trim the   sail,   al - le -

lu -   ia;   Mi - chael,   row   the boat a -   shore,   al - le -
lu -   ia;   Sis - ter,   help   to trim the   sail,   al - le -

(Optional harmony)

lu -   ia.
lu -   ia. *Fine*   2. Sis - ter,

We Are Climbing Jacob's Ladder

African-American Spiritual

Allegretto

1. We are climb-ing Ja-cob's lad-der; we are climb-ing Ja-cob's lad-der; We are climb-ing Ja-cob's lad-der, chil-dren of the Lord.

2. Ev-'ry round goes high-er, high-er; ev-'ry round goes high-er, high-er; Ev-'ry round goes high-er, high-er, chil-dren of the Lord.

And he dreamed, and behold a ladder set upon the earth and the top of it reached to heaven: and behold the angels of God ascending and descending on it. Genesis 28:12

Now the Day Is Over

Sabine Baring-Gould

Joseph Barnby

1. Now the day is over,
   night is drawing nigh.
   Shadows of the evening
   steal across the sky.

2. Grant to little children
   visions bright of Thee.
   Guard the sailors tossing
   on the deep blue sea.

If I take the wings of the morning, and dwell in the uttermost parts of the sea; Even there shall thy hand lead me, and thy right hand shall hold me. Psalm 139 : 9-10

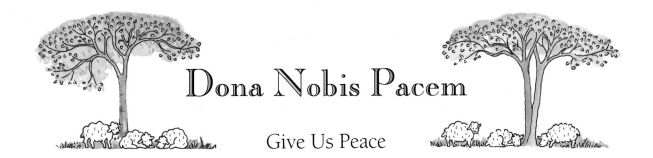

Dona Nobis Pacem

Give Us Peace

Traditional

Brightly

1. Do - na no - bis pa - cem, pa - cem;

2. Do - na no - bis pa - cem;

3. Do - na no - bis___ pa - cem;

The Lord is my shepherd; I shall not want. He maketh me to lie down in green pastures: he leadeth me beside the still waters.

Psalm 23:1-2

Do - na___ no - bis pa - cem.

Do - na no - bis pa - cem.

Do - na no - bis pa - cem.

Peace Is Flowing Like a River

Traditional

Legato

With pedal throughout

Peace is flow-ing like a riv - er, flow - ing out of you and me;____ Flow - ing out in-to the de - sert, set - ting all the cap-tives free.

If we love one another God dwelleth in us. I. John 4:12

Hope and Faith

The Lord's Prayer

Traditional

Lively

1. Our Fa-ther who art in__ heav-en, hal-lo-wed be Thy name; Thy
(2. On) earth as it____ is in__ heav-en, hal-lo-wed be Thy name; Give

king-dom come, Thy will be__ done, hal-lo-wed be Thy name. 2. On
us this day our dai-ly__ bread, hal-lo-wed be Thy name. (3. For-)

3. Forgive us our trespasses, hallowed be Thy name;
   As we forgive those who trespass against us, hallowed be Thy name.

4. And lead us not into temptation, hallowed be Thy name;
   But deliver us from all that is evil, hallowed be Thy name.

5. For Thine is the kingdom and the power and the glory, hallowed be Thy name;
   Forever and ever and ever and ever, hallowed be Thy name.

6. Amen, amen, amen, amen, hallowed be Thy name;
   Amen, amen, amen, amen, hallowed be Thy name.

Every Night and Every Morn

William Blake   Ralph Vaughan-Williams

Amazing Grace

And the peace of God, which passeth all understanding.
Philippians 4:7

John Newton

Adapted from an Early American melody

Moderately

1. A - maz - ing _ grace, how sweet the sound That _
2. 'Twas _ grace that _ taught my heart to fear, And _

saved a _ wretch like _ me. _ I _ once _ was _
grace my _ fears re - lieved. _ How _ pre - cious _

lost but now am _ found; Was _ blind but _ now I
did that now grace ap - pear The _ hour I _ first I be -

see. _
lieved. _

Open My Eyes That I May See

Clara H. Scott

Clara H. Scott

I waited patiently for the Lord; and he inclined unto me, and heard my cry. Psalm 40:1

3. Open my mouth, and let me bear gladly the warm truth ev'rywhere;
Open my heart, and let me prepare love with your children so to share.
Silently now I wait for Thee, ready, my God, Your will to feel;
Open my heart, illumine me, Spirit divine.

I Sing a Song of the Saints of God

Lesbia Scott   John H. Hopkins

Moderately fast

1. I sing a song of the saints of God,___ Pa-tient and brave and
(2. They) loved their Lord so___ dear, so dear, And His love___ made them

true, Who___ toiled and___ fought and lived and died For the
strong; And they fol-lowed the right, for Je - sus' sake, The___

Lord they_ loved and knew. And one was a doc - tor, and one was a queen, And_
whole of their good lives long. And one was a sol - dier, and one was a priest, And_

one was a shep - herd - ess on the green. They were all of them_ saints of
one of them tamed a___ great wild beast. And there's not_ an - y rea - son,

God, and I mean, God will - ing, to be one, too. 2. They
no, not the least, Why I should - n't be one, too. *Fine*

All thy works shall praise thee, O Lord;
and thy saints shall bless thee. Psalm 145:10

Rise and Shine

Traditional

With spirit

mf

1. Rise_ and shine_ and give God the glo-ry, glo-ry. Rise_ and shine_ and give God the glo-ry, glo-ry.

Rise and shine and give God the glo-ry, glo-ry, Chil-dren of the Lord.

To go to additional verses (2. The)

Last time

2. The Lord said to Noah, "There's gonna be a floody, floody."
   The Lord said to Noah, "There's gonna be a floody, floody.
   Get your children out of the muddy, muddy,
   Children of the Lord."

3. Noah, he built him, he built him an arky, arky.
   Noah, he built him, he built him an arky, arky.
   Made it out of hickory barky, barky,
   Children of the Lord.

4. The animals, they came on, they came on by twosies, twosies.
   The animals, they came on, they came on by twosies, twosies.
   Elephants and kangaroosies, roosies,
   Children of the Lord.

5. It rained and rained for forty daysies, daysies.
   It rained and rained for forty daysies, daysies.
   Nearly drove those animals crazy, crazy,
   Children of the Lord.

6. Noah, he sent out, he sent out a dovey, dovey.
   Noah, he sent out, he sent out a dovey, dovey.
   Sent him to the heavens abovey, abovey,
   Children of the Lord.

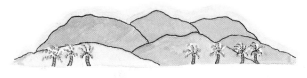

7. The sun came out and dried off the landy, landy.
   The sun came out and dried off the landy, landy.
   Everything was fine and dandy, dandy,
   Children of the Lord.

8. This is the end, the end of my story, story.
   This is the end, the end of my story, story.
   Everything is hunky-dory, dory,
   Children of the Lord.

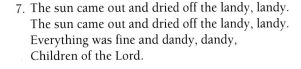

This Little Light

Traditional

Lively

1. This lit-tle light of mine,___ I'm gon-na let it shine.
2. Ev'-ry-where I go,___ I'm gon-na let it shine.

This lit-tle light of mine,___ I'm gon-na let it shine.
Ev'-ry-where I go,___ I'm gon-na let it shine.

light a candle,

Neither do men

and put it under a

bushel,

but on a candlestick;

This lit-tle light of mine, I'm gon-na let it shine, let it
Ev'-ry - where I go, I'm gon-na let it shine, let it

D.C. al fine

shine, let it shine, let it shine!
shine, let it shine, let it shine! *Fine*

and it giveth

light

unto all

that are

in the house.

Matthew 5:15

The Lone Wild Bird

Henry Richard McFayden

Southern Harmony

Quietly

Verse

1. The__ lone wild_ bird in loft - y__
(2. The)_ ends of the earth are in your_

Melody

flight is__ still with_ you nor_ leaves your sight. And_
hand; The_ sea's dark,_ deep, and_ far off land.

Chorus

I am__ yours;_ rest in__ you. Great_ Spir - it__

come, and rest in me._____ 2. The _

But they that wait upon the Lord shall renew their strength; they shall mount up with wings as eagles. Isaiah 40:31

48

Love

and

Thanksgiving

Make Channels

Richard Chenevix Trench

Orlando Gibbons

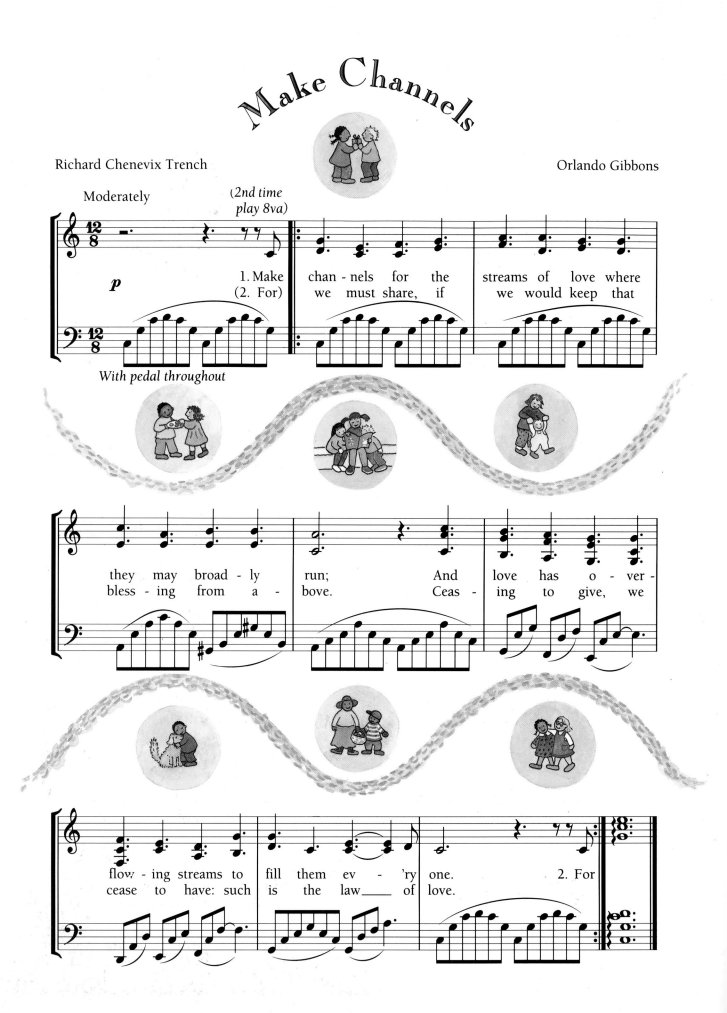

Moderately

(2nd time play 8va)

p

1. Make chan - nels for the streams of love where
(2. For) we must share, if we would keep that

With pedal throughout

they may broad - ly run; And love has o - ver -
bless - ing from a - bove. Ceas - ing to give, we

flow - ing streams to fill them ev - 'ry one.
cease to have: such is the law____ of love.

2. For

Hine Ma Tov

How Good It Is

Psalm 133:1

There are, it may be, so many kinds of voices in the world, and none of them is without signification.
I Corinthians 14:10

Israeli Round

Brightly
1. *May be sung as a two-part round*

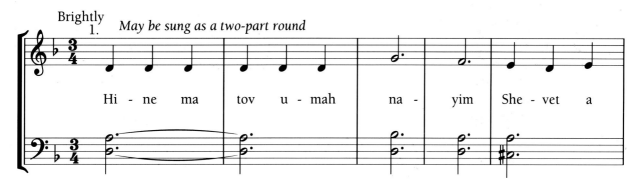

Hi - ne ma tov u - mah na - yim She - vet a

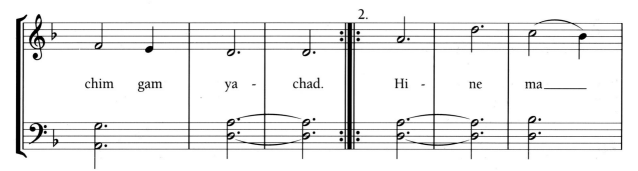

chim gam ya - chad. Hi - ne ma____

tov She - vet a - chim gam ya - chad.

Translation:
How good and pleasant it is
For neighbors to dwell together.
Good and pleasant
For neighbors to dwell together.

Come Dance and Sing

Shaker Round Dance

With spirit

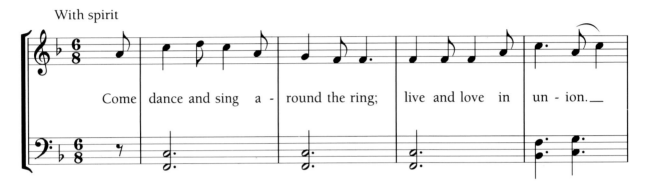

Come dance and sing a - round the ring; live and love in un - ion.

Dance and sing a - round the ring; live in sweet com - mu - nion.

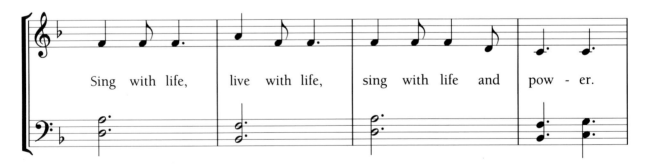

Sing with life, live with life, sing with life and pow - er.

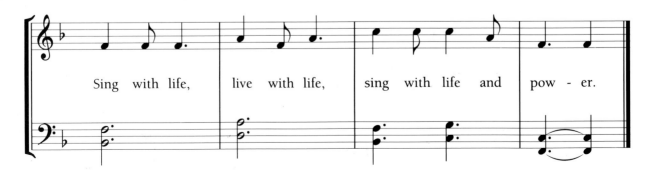

Sing with life, live with life, sing with life and pow - er.

Hop Up and Jump Up

Shaker Song

Lively

Hop up and jump up and whirl 'round, whirl 'round; Gath-er love, here it is,

all 'round, all 'round. Here is love, flow-ing 'round; catch it as you whirl 'round.

Reach up and reach down, here it is, all 'round.

53

I Would Be True

Howard A. Walter

Joseph Y. Peek

Adagio

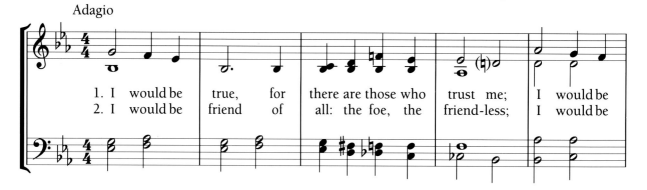

1. I would be true, for there are those who trust me; I would be
2. I would be friend of all: the foe, the friend-less; I would be

pure, for there are those who care; I would be strong, for
giv - ing, and for - get the gift; I would be hum - ble,

Finally, brethren,
whatsoever things are true, whatsoever
things are honest, whatsoever things are just,
whatsoever things are pure, whatsoever things
are lovely, whatsoever things are of good report;
if there be any virtue, and if there be
any praise, think on these things.
Philippians 4:8

there is much to suf - fer; I would be brave, for there is much to
for I know my weak - ness; I would look up, and laugh and love and

dare; I would be brave, for there is much to dare.
lift; I would look up, and laugh and love and lift.

Shining Day

The flowers appear on the earth; the time of the singing of birds is come and the voice of the turtle is heard in our land. Song of Solomon 2:12

Jan Struther

Johann Georg Ebeling

Moderately

1. We thank you, Lord of Heav - en, For all the joys that greet us, For
2. For swift and gal - lant hors - es, For lambs in pas - tures spring-ing, For

all that you have giv - en To help us and de - light us In
dogs with friend - ly fa - ces, For birds with mu - sic throng - ing Their

earth and sky and seas. The sun - light on the mead - ows, The
chan - tries in the trees. For herbs to cool our fe - vers, For

56

rain-bow's fleet-ing won - der, The clouds with cool-ing shad - ows, The
flow'rs of field and gar - den, For bees a-mong the clo - ver With

stars that shine in splen - dor, We thank you, Lord, for these.
sto - len sweet-ness lad - en, We thank you, Lord, for these.

Come, Ye Thankful People, Come

Henry Alford
Anna L. Barbauld

George J. Elvey

Slowly and flowingly

1. Come, ye thank-ful peo-ple, come; Raise the song of har-vest home.
2. All the bless-ings of the field; All the stores the gar-dens yield;

With light pedal throughout

All is safe-ly gath-ered in Ere the win-ter storms be-gin.
All the fruits in full sup-ply, Rip-ened 'neath the sum-mer sky;

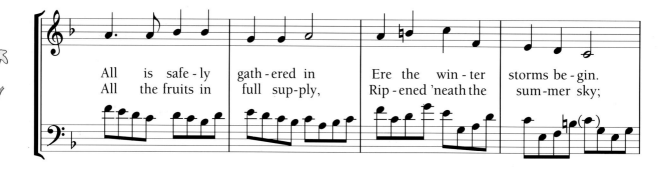

God, our mak - er, doth pro - vide For our wants to be sup - plied.
All that spring with boun - teous hand Scat - ters o'er the smil - ing land;

Come to God's own tem - ple, come; Raise the song of har - vest home.
All that lib - 'ral au - tumn pours From her rich, o'er - flow - ing stores.

life that en- | folds us, and | helps and heals and | holds us, And
those of all | ra- ces, all | times and names and | pla- ces, We

D.C.

leads be-yond the | goals which our | fore- bears once
pledge our-selves in | fel - low-ship | firm - ly to

stand.

But if we walk in the light, as he is in the light, we have fellowship one with another.

I. John 1:7

'Tis the Gift to Be Simple

Traditional

Shaker Song

When true sim-plic-i-ty is gained, To bow and to bend we shan't be a-shamed; To turn, turn, will be our de-light, Till by turn-ing, turn-ing, we come 'round right. _____ 'Tis the

in the abundance of peace. Psalm 37:11

63